NIGERIA DEEP STATE

MY PERSONAL EXPERIENCE WITH **NIGERIA CUSTOM SERVICE** & THE **NIGERIA POLICE FORCE** IN CLEARING A 40FT CONTAINER TO ESTABLISH HOSPITAL IN NIGERIA

CHIEF DR. EMMANUEL ADETULA

Dr. Emmanuel Adetula

This book was printed in United States October 2017

To order additional copies of this book:

Available at: https://www.amazon.com
https://www.amazon.co.uk

Write to:

Emmanuel Adetula

Mailing: **TULALUM HOUSE**
Challenge to Iwo Road –Ibadan Lagos/Ibadan Express Road
Before Olomi –Academy Overhead Bridge
P O BOX 39299 Dugbe, Oyo State, Nigeria
E-mail: yahumedical@gmail.com
Website: www.yahumedical.com

ABOUT THIS BOOK

Nigeria Deep state is more powerful than the government of Nigeria. This book is about my own experience of spending N3,000,000 (three million naira) in custom clearing of a 40ft container containing hospital beds and hospital mattresses imported to Nigeria by my company "YAHUTULA MEDICAL LTD" in 2017 to establish a new hospital in Nigeria. My experience narrated in this book is an evidence that the business of importation and clearing of goods at Nigeria Ports as it currently runs in Nigeria is a huge turnoff for any serious Nigerian in Diaspora who desire to come back home to invest in Nigeria economy.

This book details my own experience with Nigeria deep state corruption as it involves Nigeria Customs Service, the Nigeria Police Force and my own family member collusion with the deep state in clearing this one 40ft container to establish hospital in Nigeria in 2017. The book is a written reports of my experience with Nigeria agencies set up within the parameter of neoconservative agenda , but these agencies continue to reject a new progressive agenda of the current dispensation and the 21st century global economic order for the benefits of the Nigerian citizens.

I author more than 20 books in the past , Books like Nigerian in America and Audacity of Nigeria Revolution You can search and order any of my books including this one " Nigeria Deep State" in Paperback, Electronic format and Kindle editions. Available at:

https://www.amazon.com   https://www.amazon.co.uk

Dr. Emmanuel Adetula

CONTENTS

NIGERIA DEEP STATE

WHAT IS A DEEP STATE?

The term "deep state" implies the existence of a premeditated effort by certain government employees to secretly manipulate or control the government without regard for the policies of National Assembly or the congress or the President or the democratically elected political leaders who came to public office to make the changes promised the electorates.

The concept of a deep state – also called a "state within a state" or a "shadow government" is always a roadblock to all political campaign promises to the people of Nigeria of which I have come to discovered in my own case with motives to establish a hospital in Nigeria as my own contributions responding to the needs of Nigerians in Nigeria.

The deep state players operates with the purpose of undertaking clandestine acts to preserve the old governmental structure, they are the unelected "shadow government" operating behind the scenes of a democracy. which means that the democratic process in Nigeria today is a façade, a reason politicians will always found it very difficult to make a meaningful changes to the corruption going on in government agencies like the Nigeria Custom Service and the Nigeria Police Force , These agencies were set up within the parameter of neoconservative agenda that continue to reject a new progressive agenda of the current political dispensation and the 21st century global economic order for the benefits of the Nigerian citizens.

Nigeria deep state is a group comprised exclusively of government entities, "a hybrid association of elements of Nigerian government and parts of top-level government departments, ministries, finance and industry that is effectively able to govern the Nigeria without reference to the consent of the governed as expressed through the formal political process." They operate in collusion with retired members of the deep state, those who have graduated from this same deep state into private business and industry.

NIGERIA DEEP STATE

Nigeria deep state is not "a secret, conspiratorial cabal; it is a state within a state which is hiding mostly in plain sight, and its operators mainly act in the light of day and in most cases wearing government tax payers uniform, It is not a tight-knit group that has no clear objective. Rather, it is a sprawling network, stretching across the government and into the private sector, shielded by religious/spiritual leaders and traditional rulers, and this deep state is very powerful than the politicians who were elected by the people to office with sincere heart to help the masses, that is why under the current political dispensation it is difficult for politicians to deliver their promises to Nigerians because of the Nigeria deep state with lifelong membership unto retirement age " Change! , Change!!, Change !!!. but you cannot change a deep state Mr. President or Mr. Governor, the deep states operates and exists to take salary from the government and also to also use their uniform to collect more money as bribes from the citizens. Any attempt by any newly elected democratic government to challenge the power of the deep state is met with a force of deep state unions and association's threat for industrial strike actions.

Nigeria democratically elected government under the current constitution has become a place where the politicians survives by using the deep state to collect taxes/revenue for government programs and projects to benefits the electorate , but to be successful in revenue collection and protection of law and order, the Nigeria government has to allow the members of the deep state to freely collect bribes from the same citizens , the deep state collects money for government and collect money from themselves, despite the fact that the revenue collected for the government are in turn used as salary to pay the same revenue collectors. They are not satisfied with their own salary, so they turn to the rest 98% of Nigerians who are self employed with no pensions or retirement benefits from Nigeria government. The deep state members more money on top of their salary from these 98% of Nigeria people who have nowhere to go for help rather than go to Churches and mosques and when they got to religious services, they have to bribe God with tithes if they want God financial blessing.

Nigeria country has become a country where civil servants and uniform officers in collusion with union leaders has now become more powerful than elected state governors, Union leaders in Nigeria have the power to block politicians policies and legislative agenda because Nigeria deep state over the years acquisition of unwarranted influence, whether sought or unsought, has play their game through acts of military coups and private assassinations of figures who were seen as hostile to the old establishment. Nigeria Customs Service and the Nigerian Police corruption, bribery and forgery' is arguably the armpit of corruption in Nigeria - the most populous black nation on earth. Nigeria Custom Service and Nigeria Police Force is one of the problems of elected progressive's government who came to office with desires to make changes in Nigeria Social, economic and political order.

By its own admission, Nigeria Custom Service has two major functions: the "core" and "others". The core functions, which are just two, are "collection of revenue i.e. import and excise duties and accounting for same", and "prevention and suppression of smuggling".

But has the service Nigeria Custom Service been more of "bribe" collection than "revenue" collection. "Accounting" for revenue collection is also out of question. Although, over the last few years, the service has regularly declared a figure in the realm of Trillions as annual revenue generation, there are no documents in public domain by which the service can be held to account and by my own experience in clearing my own 40ft container from the ports in July/August 2017 nothing has change in Nigeria despite President Buhari ordered probe of all revenue-generating agencies, including Customs because the Deep state is more powerful than the Buhari government. If Buhari administration failed, it failed because of Nigeria Deep State over the year's acquisition of unwarranted influence, whether sought or unsought.

Has Customs been preventing and suppressing smuggling? Surely not to the extent that it can, because when inspection officers only "look" at a container, collect N1,000 and move on to the next container, there can't be watertight blockade against the smuggling of illicit goods or even arms into the country as you will found in my own experience of importing a 40ft container containing hospital beds to Nigeria in 2017.

Money flows up the chain of command through the informal but widespread system of returns in which subordinates pay their superiors a portion of the money they make from bribes and extortion. Subordinates often pay their superiors to be assigned to positions where they have ample opportunities to extract money from the public. Superior officers frequently set monetary targets for subordinates assigned to these lucrative posts and remove those who fail to meet their targets. Money continues up the chain of command as officers who take returns from their subordinates pay their superiors in turn. This corrupt system of returns not only encourages low-level custom and police officers to commit abuses as a means of extorting money, and effectively punishes those who do not, but it also creates a strong disincentive for senior officers who personally benefit from the system of returns to hold their subordinates accountable for extortion and other abuses.

Through years of neglect and marginalization under military rule, followed by rapid expansion leading up to and during Nigeria's civilian administrations, the custom officers and the police force in Nigeria has grown into an inefficient and notoriously corrupt institution that is largely unaccountable to the citizens it is intended to serve.

THE CUSTOMS CLEARING AGENTS

Most of the Custom Clearing Agents at Tin Can Island , Apapa-Lagos from my own experiences as narrated in this book operates within the parameter of obtaining money by false pretences, forgery, possession of illegal documents , stealing and criminal Beach of Trust. under the pretence of providing clearing services, their business is full of conspiracy with custom and shipping company officials, obtaining money from importers by pretext and stealing and forgery of Insurance certificates, Form M , Standard Organization of Nigeria certificate and false PRE-ARRIVAL ASSEEMENT REPORT and other documents working outside as agents of the insider government officials , these offences   contravene Sections 287 (9), (b), 314 (1), 322 and 365 (3), (f) of the Criminal Law of Lagos State 2015 (Revised) and same offence is contrary to section 311 and punishable under section 312 of the Penal Code Law". despite this laws, only one percent get punished because every junior staff reports cut backs of bribes taken to the Director`s desk. The Clearing ring Agents operates with fraudulent act by procuring the execution of a valuable document to clear my 40-feet container at the Tin Can Island Port, Apapa, Lagos and the Directors knows how the system works over the years , he came in and continue to ride his new acquisition of unwarranted influence unsought and since he have now become part of the deep state, he cannot not stop the system from running since it generates needed revenues for the government of the day, the deep state crime of extortion from Nigerians therefore is tolerated because they are agents of revenue collection for government, they are untouchable, so they collect for government and collect their own too . " Get your own bribe and give the government her own fees" a 2000 years old Roman system of revenue collection is still in practice in Nigeria in 2017". Underlying many of these abuses is a cycle of corruption driven by senior police officers who siphon off police funds at the top and enforce a scheme of collecting illicit "returns" from the money extorted by junior officers.

DAMAS GLOBAL LTD FORGERD DOCUMENTATION

I got my TELEX release of Cargo for my 40ft container on 07/17/2017 ,entered into Agency agreement for the clearing of my container with DAMAS GLOBAL LTD ON 07/21/2017 with payment of N340,000 cash to DAMAS GLOBAL LTD who reported back to me that he spent the money to obtain false government documents because my goods does not have Proforma invoice and Form M ,so according to my Clearing Agents the Nigeria Customs will auction my goods because I am supposed to get PAAR, FORM M and SONCAP certificate before I can import anything to Nigeria despite the fact that I did not obtained foreign exchange from a Nigeria bank. (I am a resident of United States 1999 to 2017, and I desire to come back to Nigeria to establish an hospital , I put hospital beds and hospital mattress inside a container with my own dollars in America, I never earned one kobo as income from Nigeria 1999-2017, and when the container got to Nigeria, Nigeria customs rules says that I cannot get the container release by customs unless my agent spent N340,000 to obtain documentation package or else no custom clearance process can take place) The process took my agent 21 days to process before he can get the debit notes from MSC Shipping Company and SIFAX ports and Cargo. DAMAS GLOBAL LTD reported back to me that he spent my N340,000 as follows:

1.   TIN Number Process for YAHUTULA MEDICAL = N10,000

2. PAAR plus Form M process and other documents process = N205,000

3. SONCAP Certificate Process = N118,800

4. Insurance Certificate to process Form M = N6,200

5. CUSTOM DUTY: The landing cost of the hospital beds was $4,750 evidenced in my receipt of purchase from GSA Auctions in United States. Now, the duty on beds is 5 per cent of the landing cost. But once the beds arrived, Customs officials claimed it was undervalued by the importer and it should have cost not less than $22,250. By doubling the landing cost, which has a receipt of purchase they compel me to pay duty on $22,250 to the government and issued me a custom assessment fee in the amount of N543,767 for shipping hospital beds to establish a new hospital in Nigeria despite the current Nigeria healthcare system.

The issued " PAAR NO: US20170759640/TOT, FORM M NO:MF20170080372 / BAO1120170006035 claimed that someone had bought the same beds for $22,250 BEFORE,   therefore if I bought mine for $4,750 despite a proof of receipt , my custom duty has to be based on someone else landing cost which has been used on record in the past. so after I paid my Agent Damas Global N340,000 to get FORM M and PAAR I end up with custom assessment fee of N543,767 (just the government official fee)

Readers of this book can confirm my reports above from DAMAS GLOBAL LTD   of NO 2 CREEK ROAD APAPA LAGOS , Licensed agents that collected N340,000 to process 1-4 documents above at Damas are:

1. OYEWOLE TUNDE = 08023662551

2. MOHAMMED ABDULAZEEZ = 08027019936

SIFAX PORTS & CARGO CORRUPTION
MSC SHIPPING-LINE CORRUPTION

Most shipping lines are owned by foreigners. And since Nigeria is an import-dependent country, importers are left at the mercy of foreign-owned shipping lines. This is what they do:

"The moment the ship bearing your goods berths, the shipping line immediately sends you a mail that you must clear your goods within three days. They expect you to clear within three days; meanwhile, it will typically take four to seven days for your container to be moved from the ship to the block stacking, where all containers are first kept,"

"On a ship, you may have 1,000 containers on it. So, imagine if your container was among the last 50, it won't arrive at the block stacking earlier than the fourth day. Yet, my container is still on the ship when my three-day notice starts reading at N12,000 per day charge from SIFAX PORTS & CARGO and $14,500 per day charge from MSC SHIPPING –LINE ,   a total of N26,500 per day charge for the next 21 days until my agent DAMAS GLOBAL LTD completed its fake documentation which he spent my N340,000 to get, before Customs issued an official assessment fee of N543,767

The consequence is that as early as the fourth day, importers are already being charged for demurrage. WHICH MEANS that before my Clearing Agent got the documentation process complete for customs , MSC the shipping company is charging me N14,500 per day demurrage while SIFAX PORTS & CARGO is charging me N12,000 per day making a total of N26,500 per day , with these my invoice and debit notes from MSC amount of N754,605 on container number MSCU8620299, BILL OF LADING number MSCUWS877055 while SIFAX PORTS & CARGO on its part debit notes to clear my container that contains only hospital beds to Nigeria amount to N702,750.15

THE AGENTS OF DRAFT

The total amount of N754,605 paid to MSC was made by me in draft not given to my agent DAMAS GLOBAL in cash, likewise the N702,750.15 was made by me in bank draft not given to my agent in cash, but these two drafts were given to my agent to submit to the bank accounts of both the MSC & SIFAX, now how does agents of draft comes into the game with the agents of importers?

"These 'agents of draft', as they are called, are connected with bankers. The draft agent enters the bank and locates his insider. The agents of drafts works with agents of importers to change the amount on the draft presented to the importer agents before the draft got to MSC and SIFAX. They move the money to a particular account, and when the money reflects in that account, they do a fresh draft from the receiver's account. By that time, the banker would have deducted a percentage of the N784,605 and N702,750.15 , say the banker and draft agent and the Importer agent both share the difference and the new draft with lower debit notes is now presented as official correct payment to MSC and SIFAX.

I sent a letter on September 27, 2017 to request from SIFAX PORTS & CARGO to investigate my own case, and the letter was courier delivered direct to Dr. Afolabi the CEO of SIFAX PORTS & CARGO, Afolabi is yet to reply me .

Invoice number : C10457462

VESSEL CODE :2017NPA017513 VOYAGER MSC SHULA NO: NW721A

Agency name: DAMAS GLOBAL LTD/ABDUL ABDUL CLEARING & FORWA

Consignee name: YAHUTULA MEDICAL

Bill of lading number: MSCUWS877055

What I am asking Barr. Dr. Afolabi the CEO of SIFAX is " Did the clearing agent actually present N702,750.15 to SIAFX , or another draft generated, and the clearing agent pocket some money in collusion with SIFAX employee? , did the clearing agent presented a draft of N702,750.15 to SIFAX for payment ? .

" SIFAX employee , bankers issuing draft and draft agents cabal set up to defraud MSC and SIFAX with importers money? Let's assume the banker changes 10 drafts in a day, and he makes N15,000, then he goes home with N150,000 in days? . That is just for one day. And do not forget, the business of importation is heavy in Nigeria, so these shady deals are always available every day. If he does that five times a week, he will be making approximately N3m a month, as a bank staff, which is multiple times his/her salary."

"The agents know how to bargain for waivers even when the importer is due for deduction. So when a clearing agent collects, say, a bank draft of N702,750 , Remember in an attempt not to be duped by my Agent I got my own a bank drafts on the amount issued by the MSC shipping agent on the debit notes/invoices and the SIFAX ports and cargo debit notes/invoice and also pay direct to Customs, so I thought I was a smart man from America, Really in Nigeria? , Hey Men, I gave drafts to my clearing Agent, the clearing agent takes the bank draft to the the draft agent who enters the bank and locates his insider. They move the money to a particular account, not to MSC or SIFAX accounts, and when the money reflects in that fake MSC and SIFAX and Custom account, they do a fresh draft from the FAKE receiver's account. By that time, the banker would have deducted a percentage of the amount , the banker and draft agent pay the correct amount to MSC and SIFAX which is lower than the amount on the invoices given to me as importer , because the invoice given to me the importer is never the correct amount but a fake invoice printed for the clearing agent by staff insider working for SIFAX to inflate invoices to importers, believe me when I tell you this my story,   most invoices to importers from the clearing agents are forge documents by staff of either the MSC shipping company and SIFAX ports and cargo and even the Nigeria Custom Service fees are forged too, the importer clearing agent in most cases are not importer Agent working for the interest of the importer for a fee but he is more of an Agent to employee of MSC, SIFAX and Custom Officers, that is why at the Custom house the place look like Ajegunle market or a civil war fronts or disaster scene, they are everywhere going in and out around the custom house negotiating bribes with Uniform Custom officers, everywhere is like a Civil war, everybody is fighting to get something for somebody and for themselves.

"The agents know how to bargain for waivers even when the importer is due for deduction. , but the agent in collusion with staff of MSC and SIFAX and NCS will never give the waiver back to the importer but share the difference with the company insider. This is one of the secrecy shrouding business activities at the Nigeria customs service, the shipping company and Sifax ports and cargo continues to inflate the cost of container clearing at Tin Can Island port Lagos- Nigeria under the nose of BUHARI government of CHANGE! CHANGE!! CHANGE!!! but BUHARI government expect foreign investors or successful Nigerians in Diaspora to come to Nigeria to affect a change in the Nigeria economy , and the inflated costs of importations of goods to Nigeria by importers is simply based on the activities of MSC, SIFAX PORTS & CARGO and the NIGERIAN CUSTOMS SERVICE. The Federal Government of have thus far lacked the political will to address these structural problems, follow through on reform initiatives, and implement effective CUSTOMS oversight and accountability in Nigeria.

EXAMINATION OF CONTAINERS
CORRUPTION BY CUSTOM INSPECTORS
EVEN NAFDAC, SSS, NDLEA ARE BRIBED FOR 'LOOKING'

"Customs may tell you that your container is on red alert and that your physical examination will not take place until another three days, because there are thousands of containers to be examined.

"You will need to pay Customs Officers bribe to come and open your container and examine; they have somehow legitimized this corruption. In my own case, the total payment was N400,000 over and above the official assessment fees . Meanwhile, shipping lines do not charge you day by day; they charge you upfront, and will collude with custom officers to delay the release so that you don't get any refund at the end of the day.

"Now, when it's time for your container to be opened, the Customs officers will tell you to open, even though they know that you actually cannot open the container yourself. Therefore, you are forced to engage the services of their laborers. But before the laborers lift a finger, they demand money – and you have to pay them. Meanwhile, this was one of the things you already paid Customs for."

So, what happens when the container has been opened? Representatives of all agencies go in to check, and each of them collects N1,000 "just for looking". During the inspection of the 25 hospital beds, "representatives of seven agencies" collected money from me that day amount to N34,000

These are Nigeria Police Force (NPF), Nigeria Customs Service (NCS), State Security Service (SSS), National Agency for Food Drugs Administration and Control (NAFDAC), Nigerian Ports Authority (NPA), National Drug Law Enforcement Agency (NDLEA), and Nigeria Agricultural Quarantine Services (NAQS).

Of course any act of corruption should worry any patriotic Nigerian. But in this case, it is not just the N1,000 but the sheer scale of the sum total of the individual collections. suppose in a day alone the inspectors who are deep states members and staff of the federal government agencies inspected 1,000 containers x N34,000 , By that calculation, the agency went home with an illegal collection of 34,000,000 which is not going to the Nigeria government account but to the private pockets of these federal government staffs, and from the duty amount paid to the government as fees , the government will turn around and pay same people salary, then who runs Nigeria government? The elected government or the deep state members in uniform?.

And it's hard for importers not to pay the bribe, because failing to pay these officers means that they won't inspect on the day, which in turn means the importer's container is moved to another location. When this happens, the importer not only pays a fresh inspection fee, he also has incurred more demurrage charge from SIFAX and MSC.
"So, these things are interwoven, "You pay N1,000 bribe to free yourself from 26,5000 a day charge from SIFAX or MSC . And if you don't scale a process, you can't proceed to the next. You see how complicated it is?"

After "looking INSPECTORS ", photocopies of my Invoice (PI) and the Bill of Lading are taken to the offices of the superiors of these field inspectors who collected money to look at my container, and has now see that it is just can fit into a 20ft container but was just put inside a 40ft container by the shipper to charge me 40ft container instead of 20ft container, and some of the inspectors even confirm that if my clearing agent has not been a fraudulent type, he would have process an hospital beds as possible duty free or for a lesser amount of duty instead of me paying to custom N543,767 duty on 25 hospital beds, nevertheless , despite their confirmation of nothing inside the container except the 25 hospital beds and the mattresses, but one by one the Bill of Lading are taken to the offices of the superiors of these field inspectors who collected money to look at my container, when they have signed – most of them also demand bribe total N18,000 to sign , then the documents are taken to the Releasing Officer who charge me N100,000 but refused to sign until she was given N10,000 for the custom release, if she did 1,000 containers a day, that is N10,000,000 million, you think her boss upstairs does not know what is going on downstairs ? DEEP STATE!

CORRUPTION BY THE RELEASING OFFICER

A truck exiting the port after clearance by the releasing officer, the releasing officer wields enormous powers, especially because he is last in the line. A "no" from him literally nullifies all payments since arrival of a container to Nigeria despite all the money paid so far by the importer, So he makes his money by claiming that the imported beds have been undervalued for $22,250 and that Total assessed amount for the declaration already paid was based on false declaration of what is found on the containers despite the facts that the container inspectors have confirm the 25 beds as the content and the releasing officer subsequently quoting a fresh, usually-unreasonable figure. He then tells me the importer to the requisite percentage of the new fee to the government or pays him a lesser fraction, if the goods must be released. Like all other importers, I

Chief Dr . Emmanuel Adetula was a victim too. A"But, all of a sudden, the releasing officer said even \$54,000 was an underestimation; he claimed the machine was worth \$80,000, and said we had short-changed the Nigerian government." Despite all of my protestations, the releasing officer insisted that 5% of \$44,500 had to be paid to the government. And although this calculation itself is calculated by the government at the rate of black market not official Central bank rate, but Nigeria Customs collect revenue based on illegal black market rate from me at the rate of \$1 to N360), Nigeria Central Bank declared exchange rate as illegal outside the banking system but when they want to calculate payment of revenue or fees from importers, Customs based their own calculations on illegal black market not the central bank official rates, moreover the Releasing Officer was far from interested in generating revenue for the government. She is not concern about the government fees but what is important to her is the reports of money made today to the boss upstairs.

"The tricky part is that if I didn't pay the N120,000 on top of the N543,767 already paid fee by 4pm that day, I would not only pay N120,000 the following day, I would miss the following day's deadline for moving my container, which would mean paying extra terminal and shipping charges of additional N26,5000 to both SIFAX and MSC.

Eventually, the Releasing Officer let me go after collecting – wait for it – a paltry N30,000 after I bypass my clearing agent to talk to him myself. I have to negotiate with this lady who demanded N120,000 from me inside her office at the custom office around 12 noon, she finally agreed to N30,000 cash by 4pm that day.

"I bought these HOSPITAL BEDS for \$4,750. But Customs already valued it at \$22,250 meaning I paid a duty of N543,767 to Buhari government instead of N85,500 which makes my hospital beds now at Ibadan about N660,000 each , making it the most expensive beds any patient can lie upon in Africa because of this fees.

CORRUPTION AT THE GATES
AT THE PORTS, 'GATE MEN' ARE POWERFUL PEOPLE

Trucks Drivers , A lineup of trucks queuing to enter the port

In most establishments, gate keepers are some of the least respected staff, as they are not considered anywhere close to the power brokers. Well, at the Apapa ports, gate keepers are so powerful. And this is why.

The various acts of corruption by officials of Customs and other agencies are all devised to capitalize on the importer's determination – at times, desperation – to adhere with strict deadlines for movement of goods out of the ports, to avoid paying demurrage. As a result, the releasing officer usually gives his final word a few hours before that deadline.

Now, due to the congestion outside the port gate, it typically takes a truck 12 hours to make its way into the port premises. So, if the men at the gate delay the entry of a truck after the agent has completed the clearing, this deadline can still be missed, which then means all previously-paid bribes have virtually come to naught.

By Monday August 14th, I have got Container release from the Custom and MSC, negotiated N180,000 with a Truck Driver for the transportation to Ibadan , the only thing left was for the Truck Driver to pick up Container from SIFAX Storage and come to deliver at Ibadan, so I left my own Son MICHAEL OLUWAFEMI ADETULA in Lagos to finalize the release from SIFAX PORTS & CARGO , and I came back to Ibadan to await the container , BUT my Agent DAMAS GLOBAL LTD called me with information that he has terminated the agency agreement and refused to sign the TDO for SIFAX release unless he is paid an additional cash of N150,000 or else the container can remain with SIFAX for the next 100 years at N26,500 demurrage with both SIFAX and MSC. and my SON have to secured a new agent " ABDUL ABDUL Clearing & Forwarding Agent Ltd to complete the 2% rest of the job after 98% have been done by DAMAS GLOBAL LTD former clearing agent who withdrawn his services because of my personal involvement to reduce customs bribes from about N200,000 to just N58,000 to get it done myself, at it been I did not get involved talking to Custom Officers myself, DAMAS would have told me Customs collected from him N200,000 , so doing it by myself was a loss to my Agent for about N150,000, and so TUNDE refused to sign the TDO because this American Guy is too smart for him, a reason he terminated his agency after 98% job has been completed , that was why my Son I thought all job has been completed came in to secured the help of another Agent to sign the TDO , you can reach ABDUL ABDUL new agent at Shop 72, Tafawa Balewa Square Terrace wing Race - Course, Lagos 080337895888, 08098580001 adbulabdulclearingagentltd@yahoo.com

FEMI said he had to "tip the gate man for him to quickly sign my papers, because if he didn't on time, I would have missed that deadline".

That is just one aspect of corruption at the gate. The second happens in front of the gate, where trucks are lined up and each one is in a hurry to be the first to enter. To manage this commotion, Customs engaged a team of soldiers, police, civil defense and navy to organize the truck drivers into a single line.

"When I handed our papers to a truck driver, Femi told me, 'Look, this paper expires tomorrow and you're bringing it at 6pm today. If you really want to move your container, you have to pay us N30,000 for facilitation'. That fee is outside the N200,000 we were to pay to him for moving the container from Apapa to Lagos Island.

" My son FEMI said to me, ' He did give these officers something, so that they would pass our own truck and pilot us straight to the gate'. My paper was to expire by 12 noon the following day, so it was either he paid this N30,000 bribes, or I would have to pay fresh terminal and shipping charges that would be roughly N26,500"

As usual, Femi said he paid the bribe, and he watched as a soldier collected the money and hopped into the truck to sit by the driver, directing him to head towards the gate. When the driver reached the points that were policed by the navy, police and civil defense officers, he paid them money each. In a matter of minutes, the N30,000 had vanished and the truck was right inside the port. Yet, this same truck would have been denied entry, despite holding papers clearly stating that . FEMI claimed he spent on behalf of YAHUTULA MEDICAL LTD in a single day on August 15, 2017 the following amount :-

a. SIFAX EXTRA DEMMURRAGE CHARGES after the first invoice of N632,250.15 was paid by me   = N70,500

b. BRIBE GIVEN TO SIFAX STAFF TO WRITE DEMMURAGE CHARGES =N2,000

c. BRIBE GIVEN TO BANK STAFF TO WRITE DRAFT FOR SIFAX =N3,000

d. BRIBE GIVEN TO CUSTOM OFFICERS TO SIGN TDO & EXAMINATION SHEET= N8,000

e. BRIBE TO CUSTOM OFFICERS TO GET CONTAINER OUT OF GATE =N30,000

f. BRIBE TO A NEW AGENT ABDUL ABDUL CLEARING AGENT TO COMPLETE THE JOB ABARDON BY DAMAS GLOBAL LTD = N20,000

g. AMOUNT PAID TO NEW AGENT FOR 2 DAYS JOB LEFT =N20,000

h. BRIBE TO CHANGE ADDRESS FROM DAMAS GLOBAL TO YAHUTULA MEDICAL NEW ADDRESS = N4,000

THE DEEP STATE (VS) NIGERIAN PEOPLE

Importers and Freight Forwarders have continued to lament over the billions Terminal Operators and Shipping Companies are making out of strangling terminal and service charges they impose on importers. Though the concessionaires claim to be collecting their statutory charges as contained in the concession agreement, high demurrage charges stand out as rather inflationary and to some extent illegal. Take the grossly underreported problem of incessant cyber network failure at the terminals, where agents sometimes waste up to 1 week for network to stabilize and for Nigerian Customs Service (NCS) personnel to confirm payments before giving approval for release. Within this 1 week is the 5 days grace period allowed for cargo clearing. That means the importer has already incurred 2 days demurrage for which he must pay the shipping companies and terminal operators. For the terminal operators, demurrage charges are at the rate of N14,500 for a 40ft TEU container at MSC , while SIFAX PORTS & COARGO charges N12,000 per day. Yet confirmation of payment by Customs is just one step in the entire process of clearing. they rip huge sums of money off importers by delaying the clearing process. The other is that high demurrage costs add up to high port charges . double taxation and levies paid to government, container deposits collected for shipping companies by terminal operators are not refunded despite the efforts Importers and their agents make to return empty containers on time and in good condition. At a time when the traffic situation in Apapa and Tin-Can Island has become endemic with many container-laden trucks unable to discharge containers on record time and terminals are not large enough to receive and hold empty containers as they come, talk less of handling the overall rise in cargo throughput, the strains of high demurrage have more serious economic effect. One example is the growing syndicate of touts who forge shipping and freight forwarding documents, these touting syndicates go beyond forgery of Bills of

Lading. Their sphere of activity now extends to forgery of sensitive documents like the Pre-Arrival Assessment Report (PAAR) It is pertinent to note here that, in some cases, genuine agents engage in document forgery primarily to beat the Custom's malfunctioning network system, the terminal operator's very short grace period, and ultimately the high demurrage. This proves to be unfair to the Importers and Nigeria citizens who bear the pains of inflation at the end of the tunnel .

Price inflation for commodities in our markets derives very much from additional costs like demurrage coupled with cost price of goods, freight, and insurance. Inflation of all kinds devalues everything it infects. It reduces standard of living, promotes crime, puts pressure on government, stimulates counterfeiting and money laundering, and distorts behavior. The seaport is the gateway to the economy of every nation. Attempts to increase the overall cost of imports would certainly reflect on the unit price of all goods and services in the market. This is inimical to the welfare and livelihood of citizens of Nigeria. There is no doubt that the rising cost of goods and services in Nigeria is linked to the shylock and inflationary pricing system forced down our throats by a cartel of terminal operators like SIFAX PORTS & CARGO who must recoup their investment in their own terms.

From my own personal experience in clearing my own container, I can now say that government is contributing to the distortion of the clearing system and the on-going exploitation at the ports . According to World Bank , cargo dwell time for Nigerian ports is between 20 and 28 days against 10 to 15 days for Benin Republic, 12 to 14 days for Ghana, and 8 to 12 days for Togo. Again, data from Nigerian Shippers' Council indicate that while Nigeria has 5 demurrage-free days, Benin Republic has 10 days, and Ghana has 8.

The current Director of Customs at a time of writing this book in 2017 had seduced the present government of Nigeria since he was appointed to the position to make Buhari administration believes that his stricter terminal charges would put Importers and agents on their toes and speed up the clearing process. But there is no evidence that the clearing process had performed any better since 2006. Instead, terminal operators have continued to milk Importers of hard-earned money by means of a long list of charges numbering between 14 and 20 for port and off-dock terminals respectively and they have continues to discourage Nigerians abroad to invest back home. I did not make any money from Nigeria 1999-2017, so if I go out there in America, work for my money and elected with god intentions to give back home by establishing an hospital in Nigeria, how does that end up in a crime?.

NIGERIAN POLICE FORCE
ACT AS A DEBT COLLECTORS

My Son MICHAEL OLUWAFEMI ADETULA presented my own bank account check he completed written in his own and in his own handwriting in the name of his company "TULATECH COMPANY"   in the amount of N500,000 as evidenced in my WEMA BANK account statement on September 9, 2017 without me EMMANUEL ADETULA approval of TULATECH as payee nor me Emmanuel Adetula date approval for payment of the N500,000 on September 9, 2017, for this reason I found myself at the Oluyole Police Station from 6am to 10pm that day   which gave me the opportunity to know how Nigeria Police Force operates as the people debt collectors under the pretence of being Nigeria law enforcement agent, that day in my presence the DPO/DCO handles not less than 20 cases, and 18 of the cases were about somebody owing somebody , the Lender will bribe the police to help arrest the borrower or the landlord bribe the police to help arrest the tenant or the employer used the police to arrest the employee because of money, and at the end of the day, both the complainant and the accused person will both waste their own time together at the police station and how does the DPO or the DCO at Oluyole Police Station resolved all these cases at the end of the day in my presence there ? Police got money from the Complainant and got money also to approve bail out of the accused person and the IPO got money for drafting payment arrangement signed by both the accused and the complainant, This cash and release duties is now 80% of Nigeria Police force job at the station, resolving civil money matters, and if you pay the money you owe the complaint at the police station, the complainant will not get 100% of the money paid , because the Police will cut off tithes to the DPO, that day when it was 7pm, all officers that reported for duty were all issued guns and batons, I thought maybe there was public disturbance somewhere when officers were rushing to get guns and moving out in hurry, but when I was going home after 10pm from the police station , I saw the same police officers with Guns and Batons on street corners, junctions and everywhere there are potholes used as roadblocks stopping vehicles and okadas bike riders at check points collecting money from taxi drivers and Okada riders, this is Nigeria police Force in 2017, Debt/Tithes collectors inside the station and Gifts/offering collectors at roadsides that tells me how far Nigeria deep state is far away from civilization in 2017 .

Nigeria Police Force started in 1861 , 156 years ago as a gang of thieves in uniform with the primary purpose to protect British economic and political interests... The Nigeria Police 156 years ago accomplished this objective through the often brutal subjugation of indigenous Nigeria communities that resisted colonial occupation... The use of violence, repression, and excessive use of force, stealing and bribery started over 150 years ago by the Nigeria police, this epidemic has characterized law enforcement in Nigeria ever since until now with my own experience at Oluyole Police Station Ibadan in 2017.

The first police force was established in 1861 by the British colonial administration in the territories known today as Nigeria... This 100-man contingent was essentially a consular protection force based in Lagos, which later became known as the "Hausa Force," because they were mostly Hausa guys so-named after the ethnicity of the men recruited into the unit. Yoruba were not Police then, Ibo were not Police then, the British only expanded their reach to the east and north when they formed additional police forces comprised largely of recruits from outside the communities in which they were to be deployed., The British will put Ibo police man in Yoruba land and Yoruba Police man in Hausa land and bring Hausa Police man to Lagos, that was how the white guys rules Nigeria then, and nothing seems to have change so much in 2017. These early forces were notorious for their abuses and general lawlessness. In 1891, the consul general of the Oil Rivers Protectorate in what is presently eastern Nigeria expressed shock at the "numerous acts of lawlessness and pillage" by the police, who were commonly referred to in the eastern community then as the "forty thieves" in police uniform, there are more forty thousand thieves in police uniform in 2017. Similarly, the governor of Lagos colony acknowledged in 1897 that the Hausa Force "no doubt behaved very badly in the hinterland by looting, stealing and generally taking advantage of their positions." Collecting bribes " that was a statement from the Lagos Governor in 1897, (120 years ago) what do you have to say today about Nigeria Police Mr. Lagos Governor of 2017 after 120 years? .

In 2017 Can you tell me Mr. Oyo State Governor that **The Nigeria Police Force at Oluyole Estate where you have your house are guided by the international core values of policing with integrity, ensuring that the rule of law prevails in their actions and activities, and do operate within the principles of Democratic Policing as an institution that is responsive, reprehensive and accountable to its citizens at all times?. Talk to me now, Mr. Governor of 2017 !** . The Federal Government of Nigeria in general and the police leadership in particular have thus far lacked the political will to address these structural problems, follow through on reform initiatives, and implement effective police oversight and accountability.

The Lagos, Oyo, Ondo, Osun, and Ekiti States unlike Lagos Governor 120 years ago continues to support this national police institutionalized extortion, with a profound lack of political will to reform the Nigeria Police force to states control after 156 years of the formation of this gang of thieves agency that was establish 156 years ago to protect the King of England economic and political interests in Nigeria, Now in 2017 after 156 years the Nigerian people need a community police that will protect their own interest in their own community. **Three major <u>Governmental Agencies</u> oversee the control and supervision of the Nigerian Police Force; <u>The</u> <u>Police Service Commission</u>, the Nigerian Police Council and Ministry of interior** , These Federal government agencies in general and the police leadership in particular have thus far lacked the political will to address NPF structural problems, follow through on reform initiatives, and implement effective police oversight and accountability, THERFORE the time to disband the NPF is now and be replaced by each states police department headed by a commissioner who shall reports to the Governor and a Civilian Inspector General of Police. The idea of the federal government of Nigeria running the NPF is only fit to the waste paper basket of antiquity with my experience with this agency in 2017.

Police corruption affects nearly every Nigerian, though it disproportionately impacts Nigeria's poor. Those in precarious economic situations, scraping out a living day to day, are more susceptible to police extortion because of the profound effects that unlawful detention, or the mere threat of arbitrary arrest, have on their livelihoods. The sums regularly demanded by the police also represent a larger portion of the poor's income. Moreover, many Nigerians are simply unable to pay the bribes required for basic police services.

LETTER TO AREA COMMANDER

THE AREA COMMANDER
NIGERIA POLICE FORCE
Iyaganku, Ibadan-Nigeria

October 19, 2017

Follow up to the attached proof of payment for the sum of N450,000 to FEMI ADETULA today October 19, 2017 for the delivery of 30 hospital foam mattresses to FEMI ADETULA. I hereby make the following statement to the NIGERIA POLICE FORCE in regard to my written undertaking for the payment of N820,000 to FEMI ADETULA made at Iyaganku Police Station on September 26, 2017.

The attached proof of payment reads " money owed by EMMANUEL ADETULA " I EMMANUEL ADETULA does not owe FEMI ADETULA , I EMMANUEL ADETULA is the Founder of YAHUTULA MEDICAL LTD and FEMI ADETULA was also a Director of YAHUTULA MEDICAL LTD at a time of this incident. I owned 75% shares of this new company, because I invested N16 million in the business (from my money that I work for in America, I did not have any income from Nigeria 1999-2017) and I did suggested to all the rest 4 directors of YAHUTULA MEDICAL LTD with a letter which was copy to all my family members before the 40ft container in this case containing hospital beds and foam mattresses arrived Nigeria in 2017. The letter indicated that I want to give other directors 25% shares for N4million contribution for the company start-up capital .

FEMI ambition to own 10% capital is what motivated him to go and borrow N646,000 to invest in YAHUTULA MEDICAL LTD, his investment came in as contribution to clear this 40ft container by contribution of N500,000 on August 8, 2017 as evidenced in the WEMA BANK account statement IN THE POLICE FILE for this case, in addition to N146,000 balance payment for transportation of the container to Ibadan from Tin Can Island Lagos, then Femi claimed he gave bribes to Customs Officers, bank staff and SIFAX staff for a total sum of N147,500 to expedite action for the release of the container from the Custom and Sifax, this is how Femi got to his N820,000 contributions   as a Director of YAHUTULA MEDICAL LTD.

FEMI got involved in borrowing money to invest in YAHUTULA with the hope that he can cook up 10% interest on this N820,000 hope that   with 10% theory and argument on N820,000   he will reached the mark of 10% shares of N4 million 25% on sale for 4 directors of YAHUTULA MEDICAL LTD . He is smart enough to know that Yahutula Medical has the potential of becoming a billion naira industry in a short period of years in Nigeria, so Femi smart manipulative ambition to reach 10% ownership of YAHUTULA through fabrication of lies and distortion of facts is a FEMI self imposed ambition that crashed because his lender could not give him time because his lenders want back the N646,000 money he borrowed from them after 30 days , BUT I planned to invest my own N12million 75% shares in Yahutula without payback for 5 years 2017 to 2022.

I never agreed with FEMI ADETULA or any third party lender to FEMI for a loan pay back on 10% interest for the money FEMI borrowed to become a shareholder of my new company, I never signed any written agreement to even use my car for a loan to help

Femi got a share in Yahutula Medical, any communication to that effect presented by Femi to the police is false, FEMI wanted to secure partnership in YAHUTULA , but he does not have the financial capacity to do so, I have 7 Children and none was made a Director of YAHUTULA by inheritance rights, so the option for FEMI to take over YAHUTULA MEDICAL in the future from all my family members was to invest in the startup capital of the company , but He has no money, then he went and borrowed money, , then I came in to help him pay it back does not mean I am owing FEMI to bail him out financially, so EMMANUEL ADETULA is not owing FEMI ADETULA N820,000 in this case.

FEMI ADETULA got the police involved to help him force EMMANUEL ADETULA to pay back the loan amount of N646,000, FEMI ADETULA borrowed and the bribe amount of N147,500 FEMI ADETULA claimed he gave to others with the ambition to use it as leverage investing in my company of which he is a director at a time of such action , he wanted to be the only director out of my 7 children, so he engaged Nigeria police to force me to bow in achieving his ambition , because of his action using OLUYOLE POLICE STATION with evidence of a warrant of arrest with Nigeria court on record, I then removed FEMI ADETULA on September 25,2017 from my Company as a Director and made an undertaking at Iyaganku Police Station on September 26, 2017 to refund his money invested in the company while he was a Director, this case does not make FEMI ADETULA a LENDER to EMMANUEL ADETULA as a Borrower.

FEMI ADETULA has lost the game to be part of YAHUTULA MEDICAL because I did not hand it over to any of my 7 children for free, nobody will take over YAHUTULA HOSPITAL &

CLINICS in Nigeria by inheritance rights but only through professional career or by financial contributions. FEMI try but he failed and lost the game of becoming part of YAHUTULA MEDICAL CENTERS. therefore as an addendum to the Police undertaking I hereby stated that the only option for FEMI ADETULA to get the balance payment of N225,000 and N147,000 after collecting N450,000 today October 19, 2017 out of the N820,000 are:

To sell more 15 numbers of Foam mattresses at N15,000 for FEMI ADETULA to get paid =N225,000 making a total sum of N450,000 + N225,000 = N675,000 which is the only amount that would be paid to FEMI out of the N820,000 despite the Iyaganku undertaking of September 26, 2017.

The remaining amount of N147,500 stated below which falls under FEMI ADETULA bribes to Custom officers and SIFAX PORTS & CARGO is now under investigations and EMMANUEL ADETULA will not pay FEMI ADETULA this N147,500 until the investigations are completed by the NIGERIA CUSTOM SERVICE and the management of SIFAX PORTS & CARGO. Femi Adetula N147,500 that is now under investigations expenses are stated as following:

SIFAX EXTRA 3 DAYS DEMMURRAGE CHARGES = N70,500

BRIBE GIVEN TO SIFAX STAFF TO WRITE DEMMURAGE CHARGES =N2,000

BRIBE GIVEN TO BANK STAFF TO WRITE DRAFT FOR SIFAX =N3,000

BRIBE GIVEN TO CUSTOM OFFICERS TO SIGN TDO = N5,000

BRIBE TO CUSTOM OFFICERS TO GET CONTAINER OUT OF GATE =N30,000

AMOUNT GIVEN TO A NEW AGENT ABDUL ABDUL CLEARING AGENT TO COMPLETE THE JOB ABARDON BY DAMAS GLOBAL LTD = N20,000

AMOUNT GIVEN TO NEW AGENT FOR 2 DAYS JOB LEFT =N20,000

BRIBE TO CHANGE ADDRESS FROM DAMAS GLOBAL TO YAHUTULA MEDICAL NEW ADDRESS = N4,000

BRIBE SPENT TO SIGN EXAMINATION SHEET = N3,000

If Femi has taken POSSESSION OF the rest 20 foam mattresses BEFORE October 26, 2017, then he is just lucky to have get paid N750,000 leaving him the balance of N70,000 ONLY in cash, and such N70,000 will deliver at Iyaganku Police Station when I got back to Nigeria on delivery to me by the Police (1) The dude check of N500,000 that warranted my arrest by the police on September 13, 2017 and (2) A copy of the arrest warrant issued by the Nigeria Court by 4pm authorizing my arrest by NIGERIA POLICE FORCE from my house at Oluyole Estate by 6am on September 13, 2017 because of this N500,000 dude check.

Thanks for your time

Chief Dr. Emmanuel Adetula

www.yahumedical.com

MY EXPERINCE AT OLUYOLE POLICE STATION

I was at the Oluyole Police Station on September 13, 2017 because The DPO order my arrest and pick me up from my house by 6am, nobody attended to me until he came to the office by 1pm, as soon as the DPO saw me behind the Counter, he accused me " ARE YOU DR. ADETULA from AMERICA , in Nigeria it is a crime to issue a dude/bounced check, if I take you to court on this case , the Magistrate will send you to Agodi jail straight because in Nigeria

Judges don`t listen to accused person on the issue of bad check, No judge in Nigeria allows bails for person that issued check and do not have the money in the bank, anybody who does not have money in the bank in Nigeria and issued a check goes to jail , that is Nigeria law, this is how Nigeria courts system works in Nigeria so I let you know because this is not America, then I responded to the DPO that I have been a resident of America since 1999 and that I am not a LAWYER but I went to law school to study Dispute Resolution at Pepperdine University School of Law , Malibu-California and one of the basic principle of crime investigations is for a police officer to look at the intention of the accused person in committing an alleged crime or offence and if you take time as DPO to look at the intention behind this case of my own Son misrepresenting me to my bank account, you will know this is a Civil matter" between a father and a Son and that you should not have order my arrest, "with that my response" , the DPO got angry and he immediately call to one of his officer and order him to go straight to court and get an arrest warrant on this man, the court arrest warrant was approved by a Judge around 4pm when actually my arrest took place by 6am from my house.

I was waiting at the Oluyole Police Station behind the counter 6am to 4pm until the IPO came back with court issued arrest warrant around 4pm , and incidentally I was scheduled to travel out of Nigeria back to United States on that day, a situation which led to the cancellation of my flights that day, the IPO came back , show me the arrest warrant, did not even bother if I read it through, He just said to me Mr. Lawyer from America , this is your arrest warrant issued by a Nigeria court, which means you are now under arrest for issuing a dude check , then I request to talk to a Lawyer, luckily there was one Lawyer who came to the station to bail out a client, The Police introduced him to me, and he agreed to take up my case on N50,000 fee, Right what is my offence? The Lawyer said to me I overhead the DPO when talking to you, He is 100% right, if he takes you to court, you are going to jail, Nigeria Judges does not play with dude/bounce check, it is better for you to give the police like a gift like N20,000 and give me N50,000 then I will work for your bail if you can just give N500,000 of the dude check amount to the Complainant, With your status you do not want to go to court and allow the Judge to send you to prison straight because of N570,000 , To solve this problem now, you need N570,000, I know you got it as a Nigerian from America. What do you say, because I have other Clients to attend to on appointment waiting for me at my office, and I responded to the Nigeria Lawyer, My flight is already cancelled for today, I will extend for another 2 weeks hope to see the inside of Nigeria jails and how the system works over there at Agodi prison when the Judge sent me there when we got to court tomorrow morning.

My experience with the Nigeria Lawyer and the Nigeria police at Oluyole Police Station confirmed to me in a single day that even Nigerian court system too is under the manipulation of the Nigeria Police system to cover up police illegal arrest of Nigerian citizens over cases of law enforcement officers fabrication of lies and distortion of facts or is a fact that the Nigeria police is so influential on Nigeria court systems with their power of using Nigeria court system to perpetuate their money collectors business and Nigeria Lawyers works only for money not for the interest of the innocents or for the defense of the accused persons?.

I AM REQUESTING from the Oyo State Commissioner of Police (1) Copy of the Court issued arrest warrant on me dated September 13, 2017 and (2) Copy of the Dude Check for N500,000 (3) A bank statement that indicated that the check was returned unpaid and the writing and dates on the check that indicated that it was my own handwriting with confirmation from WEMA BANK that such the check was processed as unpaid/returned as a dude check.

Because my Son MICHAEL OLUWAFEMI ADETULA claims that he did borrowed the above stated N820,000 to invest in YAHUTULA MEDICAL LTD , and the Lender wanted his money back, I signed a blank check with no payee name or date on the check and gave it to my Son, with an instruction that there is no more money in the account, all the money that I brought from United States are gone for the hospital building renovations and clearing of this 40ft container, you continued money too as a Director, you have 2 options, sell part of the beds mattress for the hospital to get your money back or hold on to this check undated, no name on it, if mattress is not sold to help you pay back your lender, when I got back to USA September 14th, I will transfer money into the account , then you have two options, give the money to your lender or produce beds frames locally to the foams mattresses through a local welder which will give you N100,000 each for a cost of a bed, if you get buyers for such beds, then with that you can pay back the N820,000 you borrowed to contribute to establish YAHUTULA HOSPITAL, but my Son went ahead on September 7, 2017, wrote his own company name TULATECH on the check, put a date of September 7 on the check while I was at Owo, Ondo State , and he presented the check to the bank at a time that I have only N50,000 balance in the account and was already set to travel out of Nigeria on the 13th without notifying me , My Son hope I have money in the account , but thought I was telling lies that I cannot give him money until I got back to USA, though I agreed to pay back the sum of N500,000 and the N320,000 he claimed he spent on behalf of YAHUTULA MEDICAL LTD on August 15, 2017. There was no previous written agreement between me EMMANUEL ADETULA and my Son OLUFEMI ADETULA or a third parties signed by me EMMANUEL ADETULA before on the payment of this N820,000, rather than help him out since he has no financial capital to invest, so the best I promised to do is pay FEMI back his N820,000 and reduced his shares from 10% to 0% shares just like other non financial contributors directors, but in violation of Nigeria banking rules and regulations My Son MICHAEL OLUWAFEMI ADETULA presented a check he wrote IN HIS OWN HANDWRITING in the name of his company "TULATECH COMPANY" in the amount of N500,000 as evidenced in my WEMA BANK account statement on September 9, 2017 without me EMMANUEL ADETULA approval of TULATECH as payee and approval to go and cash such check on September 7, 2017, but check was returned unpaid, this is what became a case for Oluyole Police station , CAPITALIZED upon by the DPO/DCO as crime that warranted a Court issued arrest warrant and threat of jail time, of which was transferred to Iyaganku Police Station by the order of the Area Commander before I left Nigeria September 27, 2017.

I have been using WEMA BANK in Nigeria for the past 25 years and no record in any Nigeria bank for the past 33 years can say that I Emmanuel Adetula ever received a loan or overdraft from a bank , except when I was the Director of Olomi Community Bank when I signed as a Surety for Dupe the mother of Femi for a N10,000 loan, I hold 50,000 ordinary shares at Olomi Community Bank before I migrated to United States in 1998, so until I brought a container for custom clearing to Nigeria, I have never in my life have to borrow money from any individual or even banks, so the fact was that Wema bank did paid this N500,000 to my Son leaving me with a deficit negative balance of –N450,000 on September 7, 2017, when I discovered this incident of negative balance on September 7, 2017 on my account while I was at Owo, Ondo state, I call the bank and call my Son threaten them what I will do if I get back to Ibadan and the N500,000 is not returned back to the bank account, both the banker and my Son refund and pay back the N500,000 leaving me with a balance of N44,000 in the bank account as of September 9, 2017 after the bank charged N5,250 fee because of my Son action, I then decided to remove FEMI as a member of the board of Directors of YAHUTULA MEDICAL LTD with a promise to send his money to him when I got back to US, then drafted an agreement and demanded we both meet at SANYO POLICE STATION IBADAN-NIGERIA for the police to act as public official to witness the agreement of Termination of Directorship and payment back of FEMI investment of N820,000, BUT when my Son was coming to the Sanyo Police station he came with his Lawyer, the SANYO POLICE STATION on seeing a Lawyer refused to witness the agreement and said to me "This is a civil matter, police does not get involves in this type of case" and I left the Sanyo Police station that day September 12, 2017 around 7pm.

On September 12, 2017 around 10pm I received a call from the DPO of OLUYOLE POLICE STATION , because I reside and own my own property at OLUYOLE ESTATE Ring Road in the past 25 years , The DPO requested that I should come to the station, that night because a case was transferred from SANYO POLICE STATION accusing me of a crime issuing a dude check to my son for N500,000 , and I told the DPO on phone that because of security to my life vacationing in Nigeria I do not go out after 10pm in the night, so I will see him 10am second day September 13, 2017, but by 6am on September 13, 2017 an army of police filled up a car arrived at my residence , waiting at my gate to arrest me for a crime of dude/bounce check issued to my Son of which he could not cash the money on September 7, 2017, I was arrested by the Police on the order of the DPO by 6am from my house on September 13, 2017 and detained at OLUYOLE POLICE STATION , IBADAN on September 13, 2017 from 6am to 10pm as evidenced in the Court issued of illegal arrest warrant INITIATED by the Oluyole Police

Station DPO ,(a warrant of arrest issued by the High court Ibadan by 4PM after the Police arrest has been executed 6AM at my HOUSE by Oluyole Police Officers) an arrest warrant that prevented me from travelling from Nigeria as schedule on September 13, 2017 which delayed my departure for 2 weeks until September 27, 2017 which cost me unexpected expenses of $800.

MICHAEL OLUWAFEMI ADETULA Lawyer and his supposed third party lender for the N820,000 after I left SANYO POLICE STATION encouraged him to arrest me his father and bribe the Police at Oluyole Police Station that the N500,000 check was a dude/bounced check, that I issued a check to my Son knowing that I do not have money to pay him back after he borrowed money to help me paid for clearing a 40ft container containing hospital beds to establish an hospital in Nigeria of which FEMI my Son is a member of the board of directors at a time of the incident, the DCO at SANYO POLICE STATION an area where the hospital is located concluded this is a civil case, but at Oluyole police station the DCO found out an element of crime in the same case, an evidence that the DPO/DCO at OLUYOLE police station played a role of debt collector in this case under the pretence of enforcing the law against crime of dude/bounce check . My Son BRIBED Oluyole Police , influencing the Police to impound and help him to SEIZED my car and keep my car at the police station until the N820,000 is paid with interest , This event stopped me from travelling back to US same day September 13, 2017, and since I was detained by the Oluyole Police station I have to extend my stay in Nigeria for 2 weeks until September 27, 2017.

Femi claimed he gave as bribes to Nigeria Customs Officers N168,000 after the official fee of N543,767 was paid by me to the Nigeria Customs. Look at this case: FEMI claimed he borrowed money, gave the money he borrowed as bribes to Nigeria customs , then Nigeria Police Officers went to Nigeria Court to get an arrest warrant to arrest me Femi`s father for not paying his Son the money he borrowed to give bribes to Nigeria Customs Officers because Femi gave bribes to Nigeria Police Officers to arrest his own father because his father came back from USA after 18 years to spend about N8million to start YAHUTULA HOSPITAL in Nigeria in 2017 to benefit Nigerians, and Nigeria Lawyer says that is how Nigeria legal system works if I do not want to go to jail, I should just bribe myself out of the case. I am a Nigerian Citizen by birth and a US Citizen by naturalization, so I have a strategic capital to contribute to the social and economic development of Nigeria with my own money that I never made in Nigeria or got from getting contracts or working for Nigeria government, but here I have to fight with Nigerian Customs , fight with Nigerian Police bribery and corruption system and also fight with my own family to invest my own money made from outside the country to help Nigerians in Nigeria at their own terms or else Nigerian system will label me a criminal or a fraud within the parameter of fraudulent and uncivilized legal system that operates in Nigeria social, political, economic, tradition, cultural, religion and every fabrics of Nigeria society, if a Nigeria cannot come home to develop Nigeria, how is Nigeria going to survive in isolation, when the generations of my own children religious beliefs system is that God will help Nigeria in Nigeria if nobody come here to help us.

I left Nigeria finally back to USA on September 27, 2017 but Financial Enforcement Network (FinCEN) of United States distributed a rule that amends the Bank Secrecy Act (BSA) implementing regulations regarding the Report of Foreign Bank and Financial Accounts (FBAR). if a U.S. person who has a financial interest in or signature authority over a foreign financial account, including a bank account has transferred money more than a $10,000 limit at any time during the calendar year, the Bank Secrecy Act require him or her to report the account by filing a Report of Foreign Bank and Financial Accounts (FBAR) therefore I cannot transfer more money to Nigeria for the rest of the year 2017 , THEREFORE the OPTION to send to Nigeria from United States the amount of N820,000 to Femi as per my undertaking at the Iyaganku Police Station on September 26, 2017 is no longer the options in 2017, therefore the only way that MICHAEL OLUWAFEMI ADETULA can get paid his N820,000 as per the undertaking has since detailed in my letter to the AREA COMMANDER at the Iyanganku Police Station dated October 19, 2017.

On September 26, 2017 I did delivered letters to NIGERIA CUSTOMS SERVICE and SIFAX PORTS & CARGO to initiate an investigations into the clearing of the 40ft container , I paid N702,750.15 to SIFAX PORTS & CARGO and also paid N543,767 as official duty to NSC , and FEMI also my Son claimed he borrowed N168,000 to bribe the official of SIFAX and CUSTOM to expedite the release of the container on August 15th, the investigations at NIGERIAN CUSTOMS SERVICE and at SIFAX PORTS AND CARGO is to determine how and why I spent over N2.6 million in clearing a 40ft container . Femi also claimed he spent N820,000 in addition to my own N2.6 million to clear this same container making it over N3million spent to clear a container containing only " 109 hospital foam mattresses, 8 completed hospital beds and 32 bed head boards" value by customs at N8million? . This investigation should trigger a refund from NIGERIAN CUSTOMS SERVICE and SIFAX PORTS AND CARGO to YAHUTULA MEDICAL LTD

YAHUTULA MEDICAL LTD NEW MEMBERS OF BOD

(A)   I paid my business registration Agent to Corporate Affairs Commission , the sum of N43,000 on September 25, 2017 to remove all current members of Directors of YAHUTULA MEDICAL LTD and submit the first one year Audit reports to CAC. All BOD has been removed and replaced according to CAC records. New 4 members 4 BOD now consists of me EMMANUEL ADETULA and the management team who are Medical Doctor , Pharmacist and Registered Nurse. The other 3 Members of BOD shall also formed the management team to run YAHUTULA Hospital and Clinics in Nigeria www.yahumedical.com , The TULALUM HOUSE, OWO HOUSE and OLUYOLE HOUSE my freehold properties in Nigeria are now designated in my written willy as YAHUTULA MEDICAL hospital and clinic center locations, This arrangement shall be based on Memorandum of Understanding freehold lease agreement with no rent payment from 2017 to 2067 (50 years) and no member of my family shall hold shares in YAHUTULA MEDICAL LTD by inheritance and no member of my family shall belongs to the management team unless they apply through the management as a qualified candidates for vacant positions. Yahutula hospital shall be to the benefits of the general public.

(B) I have decided to employ my infinite potential with the power of my strategic capital as a US Citizen within the parameter of adventure of a lifetime to establish YAHUTULA Hospital and Clinics in Nigeria to create a vibration mark on this planet, this is now my   vision in Nigeria , This shall be done through a Memorandum of Understanding with medical professionals creating a private public partnership at local, state, federal and international level and YAHUTULA HOSPITAL will become my legacy, and any family member who takes steps to frustrate my vision because of their own inheritance ambition over Owo House, Oluyole House and Tulalum House properties does so at his or her own risk, and in accordance with my Willy and codicil to my will , my OWO HOUSE, OLUYOLE HOUSE AND TULALUM HOUSE is leased FREEHOLD with no rent payment for YAHUTULA MEDICAL CENTERS management team AND to my proposed RADIO/TV Stations management team in Nigeria from 2017 to 2067 (50 years) .

When the story of your own family has led to an evidence recorded with Nigeria Police as written in this book in FEMI ADETULA (vs.) his own father , It is time to change your own story , changing my own story is to go ahead and use my own properties in Nigeria to establish my own vision to benefit millions of Nigerians in Nigeria in accordance with my purpose and destiny , The life that God has given me is an uncommon grace of God OPEN to not more than 10% of Nigerian men on this planet, I will not be discouraged or stopped to participate in the revolutionary change needed by this country . The uncommon grace of God in my life that has guided me since 1964 will guard me to live long into old age with all my faculties intact. I know whom I am and whose I am, I know where I came from and where I am going, so my life is good, I love my life and my life is not set to benefit only my own immediate family but as a channel to bless millions of people, and the NIGERIA DEEP STATE CORRUPTION will not stop CHIEF DR. EMMANUEL ADETULA to contribute his own God given talents and gifts to the revolutionary changes needed in Nigeria at this time.

BOUNCED CHECK

The only problem in my family is lack of Money, the root of all evil in Adetula family is money, and the reason is because I have one human weakness, it is not fornication, it is not adultery , it is not immorality by your religious standard. The choice I made with my money is the foundation of my family problem, Nobody can deny the fact that I have been a very hard working young man since my youth with proof of the house I live and the Car that I drive, Looking at me outside, no one in Nigeria can say that I am a poor man in the past 33 years, but my sin is the fact that I love investing 80% of my legitimate income into real estate by denying myself and my family the desire pleasure and entertainment, so everybody that sees my estates driving by always conclude that I am a rich man who has the money in the bank but do not want to help anybody with his money.

My other weakness is that I have a bad judgment in choosing a wife, because I have the proclivity to get attracted to poor ladies, I have never had a relationship with a rich lady in my life even a university graduate or a any career woman from 1983-2017, I always choose poor woman as a friend. I was raised a poor boy since I lost my own mother as a child in 1964,so my soul navigate between poverty and women, I have no feelings of looking for a woman to help me financially or to nurse me , I am used to taking care of myself from a very young age, so I grew up with emotional attachment to poor people , particularly struggling young ladies from poor families who needed help, I always feel some kind of connections with homeless and jobless individuals when I see one, even with all the opportunity of real estate and property management given to me in America , I cut my houses into single room occupancy and rents it out to single mothers, I have this satisfaction from helping the poor women and the needy, so choosing a poor woman for relationship is natural to me, the more poor you are the more connection you have with my soul, so getting marry to a poor lady for me emanates from having the compassion to help her out from her struggling condition, I cannot walk away from a poor woman, there is this natural feelings saying to me, I wish I can do something to help her , maybe I can work with her to take her out of poverty , but every women I allow this feelings to connect me with always take advantage of my emotions , In America there are some ladies that has stay in my house for months with no sexual relationship between us, anybody outside automatically assumed something is going on between us, but the truth is She has no place to stay, and I allow her into my space, and we are friends, most of my friends are women, I feel more comfortable living , going out and be alone with women than men with no feelings or intention for sex .

This weakness of attractions to poor individuals despite being considered a rich man by public standard always makes me a victim of poverty because women with financial needs looking at the car he drive and the house he live and the work he do, hope this man will pull her out of poverty always push them into want to be in permanent relationship with me and that is what led to my choosing a poor woman as wife, a woman who brought no shoes, no bags, no clothes, no job , no career, no parental financial support to my house is the root cause of Adetula family money problem.

In the past 33 years, no woman has come into my life to give me any financial support, but as soon she came into my life with empty bag , she brought nothing to the table of the marriage, but came into the man life with the hope that he is a rich young man who will not only meet her financial needs , but also solve her family financial problems because she came from a poor family to marry this blessed young man is the foundation of all Adetula money problem .

I always end up as the only person with income in the house, so not using the 100% legitimate income to provide the needed money to my wife, but continue to invest in real estate is the root of my problem, because she came in with the hope that because of the house, the office and the cars that she saw, She hope I have money in the bank too, or the potential to have money in the future, but only to come in as a wife, had a child quickly for me and discover too late that this man looks like a millionaire outside , but after I made the decision to be his wife ,   getting inside his house as a wife only to found out too late that he has no money in the bank. He is just a poor man who cannot meet his wife needs, Now she has made a bad choice , She expected financial needs to be supplied by the husband to the wife, to her own children and also help her in laws with money gifts, even her own brothers and sisters, but the reality of discovering too late that big cars, big house or big business does not guaranteed happy marital life .

This always led to the woman facing the pressure from family and friends of the wife, why is it that your rich husband is not helping you and us out with money with all these cars, houses and offices, businesses?.

How does a woman explain that to her friends and family and the public? and what would you do ? If you have no job or career as the woman to get your own money?, Would you be going out sleeping around for money when everybody knows whom your husband is in town? .

This experience becomes a shocking disappointment to the woman family which always lead to domestic violence mix up with disrespect, dishonor of the husband and running from churches to mosques and to spiritualists to manipulate the man to give out money to the wife, if the money refused to come out of the man pocket it then leads to a little adultery here and there , which at the end of the day led to the woman getting lucky one day to get a better man who can be manipulated not to use his money for investment in real estate but spend it on his own wife and children and take care of his in laws, that is how I always loose out, so whenever matter get to that point I will get out peacefully to save my life since I have no mother or wife or family to help me fight the wife, that is why any woman who have left me will never have a story to blame me for than complains saying to everybody in town that "   She suffered , he never provide me money" and " He never provide money to me to raise my children" . " Rich man outside and Poor man inside".

Anytime another opportunity come again to get another woman, I will make the same bad judgment again based on my emotions of getting attracted to poor lady because she is poor and have nothing , I have everything it takes to marry a rich lady from a rich family or a career woman who will come into my life to help to lift me up from where I am now, but I always make the same mistake over and over again to get hook up with a poor lady who have nothing to contribute to improve me financially but come into my life to give me only private part, She came with no single briefcase of clothes brought to my house but came in with the hope of sending a briefcase full of money to her parents from this rich man in few months time, hope I have money to help her out, hope she will get opportunity to get out of poverty if she marry this man, she will quickly got pregnant for the man, because she has found a rich man, or potential to be rich and get out of poverty, this cycle is what led me to having 7 children by 4 different women not because of immorality. Any woman that left me with my children left for no other reason than money problems during the relationship, they left me with the hope to get a better man who has real money than me, If I allocated rooms for each of them in my house today, they will all come back next Christmas . if my current wife left me today, before Christmas another poor girl will move into my house, Last time I waited for 14 years as a single man, but I made the decision again , and made the same mistake , so for the past 33 years no woman who have share a house with me ever wake up in the morning and go to work and come back home with pay check as salary, but all my marital life it has always been me only working for money in the house.

In the past 33 years , No father, no Mother, No wife, No children , No Friend, No brother, No Sister and No family member has ever come to me to give me money, but everybody has come to demand money from me, and all of them has curse me out for not having enough money from me, even Pastors, Evangelists, Prophets and Prophetess always get angry with me for not giving enough offerings or pay them no tithes, all anger against me by everybody are based on the fact that I used 80% of my earned income to develop real estate instead of spending it to be popular and famous with everybody which is an interpretation of selfishness.

At a time of writing this book in 2017, I have 7 Children, 6 males and I female, 4 in Nigeria and 3 in United States 7 from 4 different women. Dupe divorced in 1996 got remarried after the divorce to another man and had a daughter for this other man despite having YEMI, FEMI and BOLADE for me, Temitayo left in Nigeria with 6 months old baby ABIYE in 1998 when I travelled to United States left to get married to ADENIJI and now have children for the other man, She is now Mrs. Adeniji , though Dupe still maintain her name as MRS DUPE ADETULA a notion encouraged by YEMI her Son, I hope DUPE will soon change to the new husband surname.

Today my grown up children YEMI, FEMI, BOLADE and ABIYE in Nigeria story is built around money relationship and property inheritance sermons ; Our mother raised us, we struggle to raise ourselves without your money, so you deserved to be dishonored , disrespected as a father because you have money but refused to give us your money. Even my own Brothers and Sisters , family member's problems with me centered on money, he is in America, he has money with all these properties everywhere, he does not want to help anybody, he has money, and he cannot give his money to us. Money is the root of all evil in Adetula family, Even Prophets and Pastors want money from me too, I cannot get a free prayer session , if I am ready to give, my charges are set higher than others, and when I paid the requested fees for anointed olive oil, soap, candles , perfume and handkerchief , they will ask me to make vows for more if my prayers got answered, Everybody believes I kept the money in the bank , and when FEMI my Son got my check, he presented a check of N500,000 to the bank and the check bounced.

FEMI my Son went to the Police with his mother and BOLADE his junior brother and his Senior brother YEMI encouraged him to fight this evil man with all he got to get money from him, YEMI , FEMI, BOLADE and their mother DUPE made an attempt using NIGERIA POLICE and the COURT to get money from him " RICH MAN OUTSIDE, POOR MAN INSIDE was Dupe nickname for me since 1985, so when this money, money thing get to the Police Station, I end up with making an undertaking with the Police to send my money kept at the Bank of America to them in Nigeria, but money did not come from America bank , and since there is no money in Nigeria bank , Femi has to sell foam to get money in Nigeria for his bounced check and I still keep my Real Estate which I invested my legitimate income to possessed 1993-2017 in Nigeria, the cost of blocks and cement at time I built these house was the same cost of ice cream blocks then, I could have used it for Pizza then and have nothing today, and end up living at YEMI or FEMI house by now anytime I vacation in Nigeria. Despite the facts that I have properties, home and office both in USA and in

Nigeria my own Son is arresting me with police, suppose I have nothing and take a room in his own house, What will he do to me?

Nigerians Christian believes interpretation of a man of integrity is a man married to one woman for 33 years, but my marital life was not fortunate to meet this Nigerians interpretation of a man of morality and integrity in that respect, Nevertheless, any young Nigerian Lady of 33 years old like my new Nigerian wife here with me in United States with legal residency to work and to school in America , given the opportunity to raise our US Citizens children here in America has been given enough by me to take care of herself and her own children , even her own parents without much dependency on her husband financially for the rest of her life. She is positioned in America to build her own house both in USA and in Nigeria, so my building properties in Nigeria are not her inheritance focus, so it is very convenient for me to willy all my Nigerian properties for public use as stated in my Willy and not for any family children inheritance fight in the future. so the story now ends that as per the properties of OWO HOUSE, OLUYOLE HOUSE AND TULALUM HOUSE it is now established in my willy as freehold lease for 50 years 2017-2067 to YAHUTULA HOSPITAL and my proposed RADIO/TV Projects to establish my legacy in Nigeria.

NIGERIA BLACK CAT

Black cat in Ghana symbolizes bad luck but in Peru it symbolizes good luck, A poor Ghana man migrated to Peru and He got married over there to a Peruvian woman who contributed immensely to his success and prosperity, he then wrote a letter back home to his own people in Ghana with a simple statement ,

" **My wife is a black cat in my life"** , but the Ghana people interpreted his letter within the context of Ghana tradition, custom and religious beliefs to mean **" My wife is a bad luck in my life"** as you read my story your interpretation and judgment on my Story with Femi my Son as discussed in the previous chapter will simply be based on your culture, tradition and religious believes , because   most of the decisions or choices you make in life depends on your level of soul maturity , you cannot deny a fact that however educated you are in Nigeria , whatever position you may occupy in Nigeria today or your level of success or riches in Nigeria somebody like me did know something you don`t know yet, simply because of my travelling outside Nigeria to reside in another part of the world and I have seen the world in a different perspectives, different from the way you are seeing it right now you live all your life in Nigeria,   so I have come to know that a black cat can symbolizes either bad luck or good luck depending on the country where you live.

I have come to know that a bible verse can work for you in Nigeria but means nothing to American Christian people because of their level of social, political and economic development, I have come to know that Road Safety can arrest you and impound your car for speeding 60 kilometers in Nigeria roads, but in Germany you can speed up to 220 kilometers and no police will stop you , I can make a decision about my life, family or something and not feel guilt about it why you may think you are going to hell for doing the same thing that I have done in my own life, so your choice or decision or judgment of others or the way you think is based on the fact that if you have never been to another person father's farm, the tendency for you to think that there is no farm as big as your father's farm will always be your mindset. That is why I have come to a point in my life where I am not trying to fit to Nigerians interpretation of a man of integrity but striving always to be a man of laws and equity, honesty and justice with transparency and always trying not to hurt myself to fit into the box of good reputation seekers, I maintain equity, law and order to protect myself and others in my care because a black cat is not bad or good for it all depends on what you have come to know about a black cat that others don't know.

I operate within the parameter of God grace upon my life, this grace is given by God to not more than 10% of Nigerians on this planet earth, I cannot deny this grace to make you look good, I have no regret for the way I have live my life since May 24, 1964 that my mother died and left me to survive as a child, I have no apology to offer anyone on this planet for God's grace upon my life. In this life most of the things you see with your eyes are not real, you can believe what you choose to believe, but you cannot put me in your own box that you created for people seeking public acceptance. . I did not write this book with intention to become a Nigerian politician or a Nigerian Bishop, so you cannot cage me in your BOX. The reason your Pastor is richer than your father is because your father gives to 100 people while your Pastor receives from 100 people, at the end of the day the Pastor will have cash left at the bank, not because he is more holy than your father.

When the story of your life matched up with evidence, the right thing to do is to change your story by making a decision based on the present events of your life , God is not a God of the past, God is not a God of the future, He is in the presence not on the past stories of your family or on what may happen to you at your old age or what your children may become in the future, I travelled around the world, and have to come realized that riches is nothing to a man if you do not live a long life because inheritance philosophy does not sustain a man legacy, God number one blessing to desire is for a man to live a long life , if you see something that is set to kill you and you are quoting the bible that " No weapon formed against me shall prosper" instead for you to run, then after you die ,   the   same shooter of the weapon will inherit your possessions .

For the rest of my life I am going to maintain homes and businesses both in Nigeria and in United States, Living and doing business in both countries on my dual citizenship rights , devoting my life in the service of millions of people not only to my own family and biological children, that is my found purpose and destiny as father of the fatherless, husband of the widows and the fighters for the Orphans as I now do around the world through the ministry of Christ Channel Network a 501 (c) 3 nonprofit/non-governmental organization registered both in United States and now registered in Nigeria.

Moses chose Joshua over his 2 Sons who went back with their mother to Jethro village instead of following their father to the promise land. Moses life was not playing an inheritance game with his own biological children choosing them over the plan of GOD for the deliverance of the people of Israel who share his God given vision , and just like KING DAVID in the bible I will anoint my successor before I cross over to the other side after creating a vibration mark on this planet to benefits millions of people in accordance to my vision, purpose and destiny, so I give God the glory for a good life, my life is good , I love my life, I don`t know what you think about me after reading this book, but I feel good about myself, I love what I do, establishing a legacy that will endure to generations to come AND SO-IT- IS. AMEN.

YAHUTULA HOSPITAL IBADAN OYO STATE, NIGERIA

YAHUTULA MEDICAL CENTERS

ABOUT THE AUTHOR

Chief Dr. Emmanuel Adetula holds a Nigerian traditional Chieftaincy title as the Atolosa of Ola, Osun State of Nigeria, Born in Owo, Ondo State of Nigeria, Resident at Ibadan, and Oyo State of Nigeria since 1978. Master of Arts in Divinity and Doctor of Philosophy in Social Work. He studied Philanthropy at La Sierra University School of Business, Riverside, California. Professional Training in Conflict Analysis, Interfaith Conflict Resolution, Mediation, Negotiation and Conflict Management from United States Institute of Peace Academy, Washington-DC and Pepperdine University School of Law- Straus Institute for Dispute Resolution - Malibu, California, Emmanuel Adetula is currently a Franchise Owner with Jackson Hewitt Tax Service the second largest Accounting &Tax Preparation Company in United States, Principal Associate at Emmanuel Tula Tax Service, Realtor/Property Manager at Nationwide Real Estate Executives and a Dispute Resolution Specialist at Emmanuel Tula Associates. Founding President of Christ Channel Network Inc. doing business as CCN HOUSE providing housing to low income individuals and families in the state of California since 2002. He is the current Chairman/Managing Director of YAHUTULA Medical Ltd. Emmanuel Adetula holds a Triple Citizenship; a Nigerian by Birth, a US Citizen by Naturalization, and a Citizen of Heaven by adoption. Chief Adetula. Moves to United States in 1998, back to Nigeria in 2014 to establish YAHUTULA MEDICAL CENTERS and Radio/TV Stations. He currently maintains homes and offices both in USA and in Nigeria.

Emmanuel Adetula has author more than 20 books in the past ,
Books like Nigerian in America, Audacity of Nigeria Revolution ,
You can search and order any of his books including this one, which is now available in paperback, Electronic format and Kindle editions
at   https://www.amazon.com
https://www.amazon.co.uk

Chief Dr. Emmanuel Oluwole Adetula
Chairman/Managing Director
Yahutula Medical Ltd www.yahumedical.com

YAHUTULA HOSPITAL IBADAN OYO STATE, NIGERIA

YAHUTULA CLINIC OWO ONDO STATE, NIGERIA